Super Sea Creatures

SEAHORSES

GAIL TERP

BLACK RABBIT BOOKS

Bolt is published by Black Rabbit Books
P.O. Box 3263, Mankato, Minnesota, 56002.
www.blackrabbitbooks.com

Marysa Storm, editor; Grant Gould, designer;
Omay Ayres, photo researcher

Names: Terp, Gail, 1951- author.
Title: Seahorses / by Gail Terp.
Description: Mankato, Minnesota : Black Rabbit Books, [2021] | Series: Bolt. super sea creatures | Includes bibliographical references and index. | Audience: Ages 8-12 | Audience: Grades 4-6 | Summary: "Dive into learning about seahorses with vibrant photography, engaging text, and range maps, size comparisons, and other infographics"– Provided by publisher. Identifiers: LCCN 2019026679 (print) | LCCN 2019026680 (ebook) | ISBN 9781623102852 (hardcover) | ISBN 9781644663813 (paperback) | ISBN 9781623103798 (ebook)
Subjects: LCSH: Sea horses–Juvenile literature.
Classification: LCC QL638.S9 T47 2021 (print) | LCC QL638.S9 (ebook) | DDC 597/.6798–dc23
LC record available at https://lccn.loc.gov/2019026679
LC ebook record available at https://lccn.loc.gov/2019026680

Printed in the United States. 2/20

Image Credits

Alamy: Andrey Nekrasov, Cover, 1; Dreamstime: Elena Sanchez, 23 (fins); Flickr: Kandfoto, 32; iStock: GlobalP, 31; masteroflight, 6; MediaProduction, 24; Minden: Alex Mustard, 3, 12 (top), 15 (btm), 18; Colin Marshall, 22–23; Doug Perrine, 23 (babies); Hans Leijnse, 4–5; Jelger Herder, 10–11; Shinji Kusano, 21; PINK TANK SCUBA: PT Hirschfield, 28; Shutterstock: Gerald Robert Fischer, 15 (middle); GOLFX, 8–9; Hein Nouwens, 16–17; InsectWorld, 12 (btm); irin-k, 24 (shrimp); lunamarina, 24 (fish); Macrovector, 24 (plankton); Nantawat Chotsuwan, 24 (seahorse); Prachaya Roekdeethaweesab, 24 (crab); Rich Carey, 26–27; Sergei25, 24 (larvae); travel.padi.com: Padi Travel, 15 (top)

CONTENTS

CHAPTER 1

IN THE SEA

A seahorse curls its tail around some coral. It glances about. Its left eye looks forward while its right eye looks back. When **prey** gets close, the seahorse's eyes will see it. But prey won't see the tiny seahorse. It blends right in with the coral.

A small shrimp comes close. With lightning speed, the seahorse moves its head forward. Slurp! It sucks in the shrimp.

COMPARING LENGTHS
big-bellied seahorse
longsnout seahorse
giraffe seahorse
Denise's pygmy seahorse
inches
2

Made for Ocean Life

About 50 kinds of seahorses live in the world's oceans. They're made for life at sea. Their tails are flexible and can grab things. They're great for holding onto grass and coral. Holding on helps small seahorses stay still in moving water.

Although seahorses are fish, they have no scales. Instead, they are covered in bony plates. These plates are covered in skin. Seahorse skin can change colors.

Getting Around

Seahorses use their small fins to swim. Their back fins move them forward. The two fins on their heads help them steer. They also have **swim bladders**. Seahorses change the amount of air in them to move up and down.

Seahorses' back fins move very quickly. Even so, seahorses swim slowly. They're one of the slowest fish.

SEAHORSE FEATURES

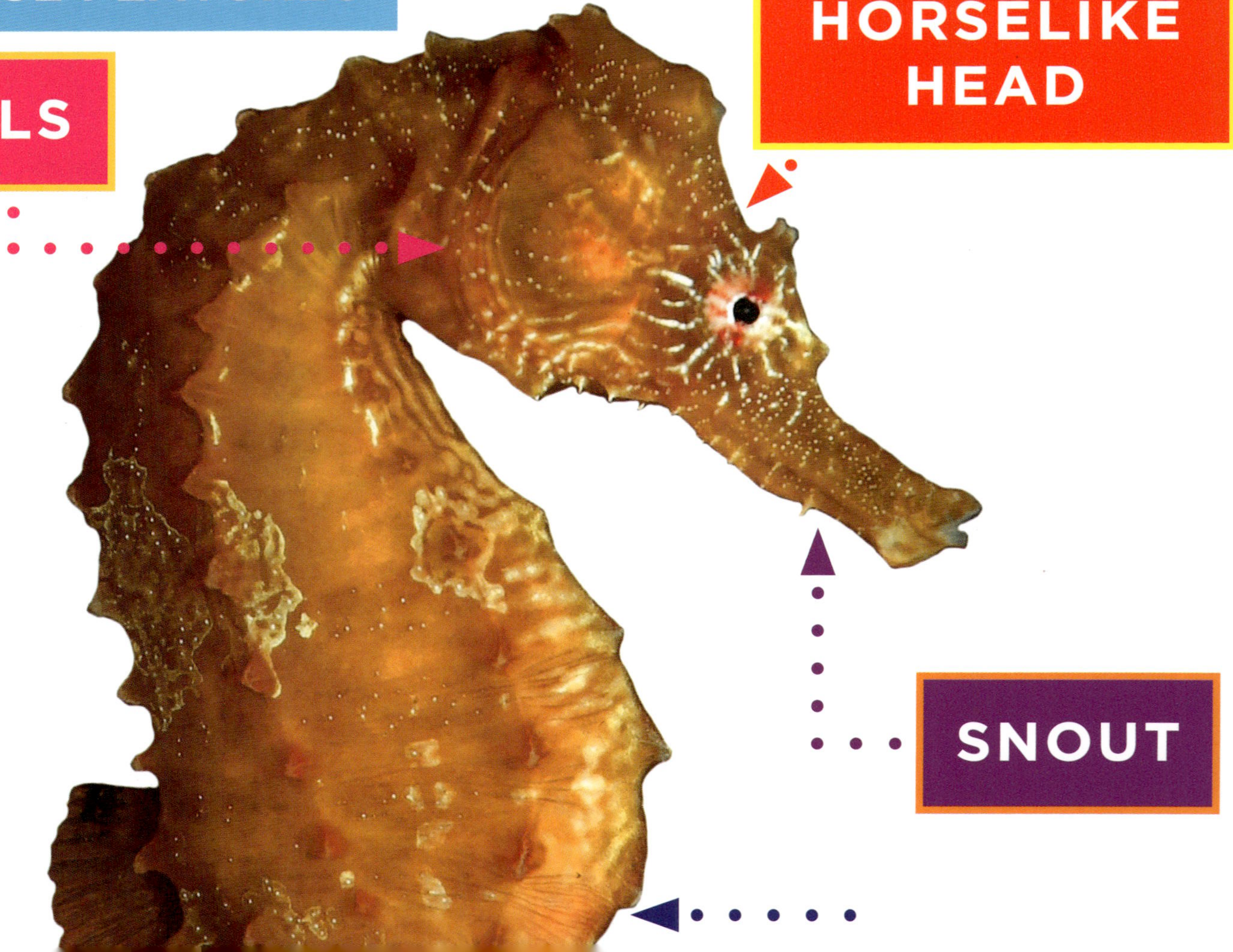

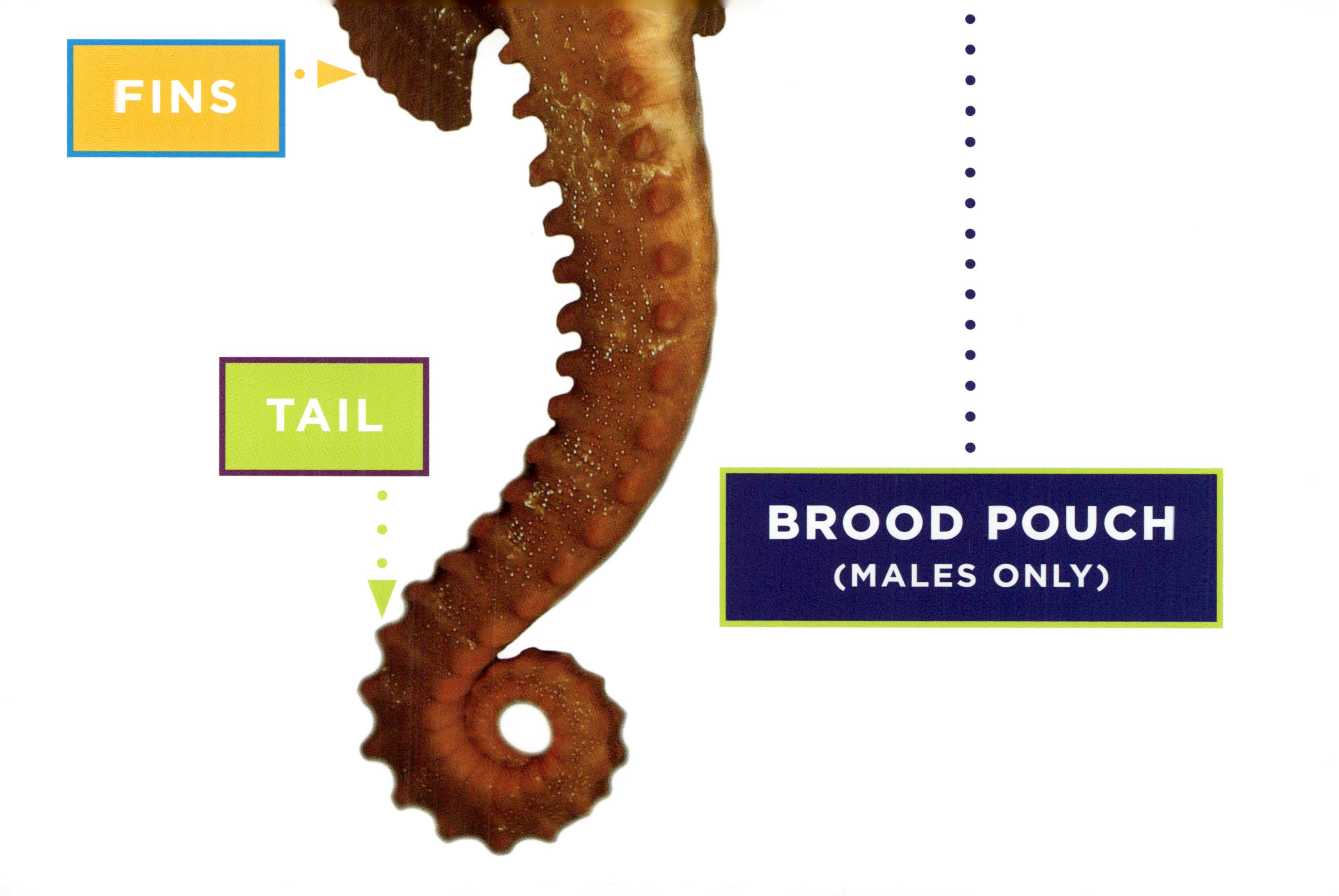
FINS
TAIL
BROOD POUCH
(MALES ONLY)

CHAPTER 2

FOOD TO EAT and a Place to Live

Because their mouths are so small, seahorses eat small prey. Tiny shrimp fit in their mouths. **Plankton** and fish **larvae** fit too. Seahorses have no teeth. They suck in prey and swallow it whole.

Seahorses don't have stomachs. That means they don't have a place to store food. They must eat all the time to stay healthy.

At Home in the Sea

Seahorses are mostly found in warm oceans around the world. They often live in shallow water near coasts. Many can be found in coral reefs. Some live among tall seagrass.

These fish usually don't travel far. Instead, seahorses stay in **territories**. They spend their days finding food in these spots.

Female seahorses have large territories. Males have smaller spots inside the females' territories.

SHALLOW WATER

CORAL REEFS

TALL SEAGRASS

WHERE SEAHORSES LIVE

Seahorse Range Map

Seahorse dancing can last hours.

CHAPTER 3

FAMILY LIFE

Seahorses spend most of their time alone. But they do meet to have babies. To have young, a female seahorse puts its eggs in a male's pouch. The male then **fertilizes** the eggs and carries them in its body.

Seahorses often **mate** for life. Every morning, mating pairs greet each other with a dance. While dancing, they might link tails. They might change color too.

Baby Seahorses

About two to six weeks after mating, the males give birth. The tiny babies are born fully formed. And they are ready for life in the sea. Their parents don't take care of them. Little seahorses must be careful. Their tiny size makes them easy for **predators**, such as fish, to eat.

up to .4 inch (1 cm)
up to 6 inches (15 cm)
1
2
3
4
5
6

BY THE NUMBERS

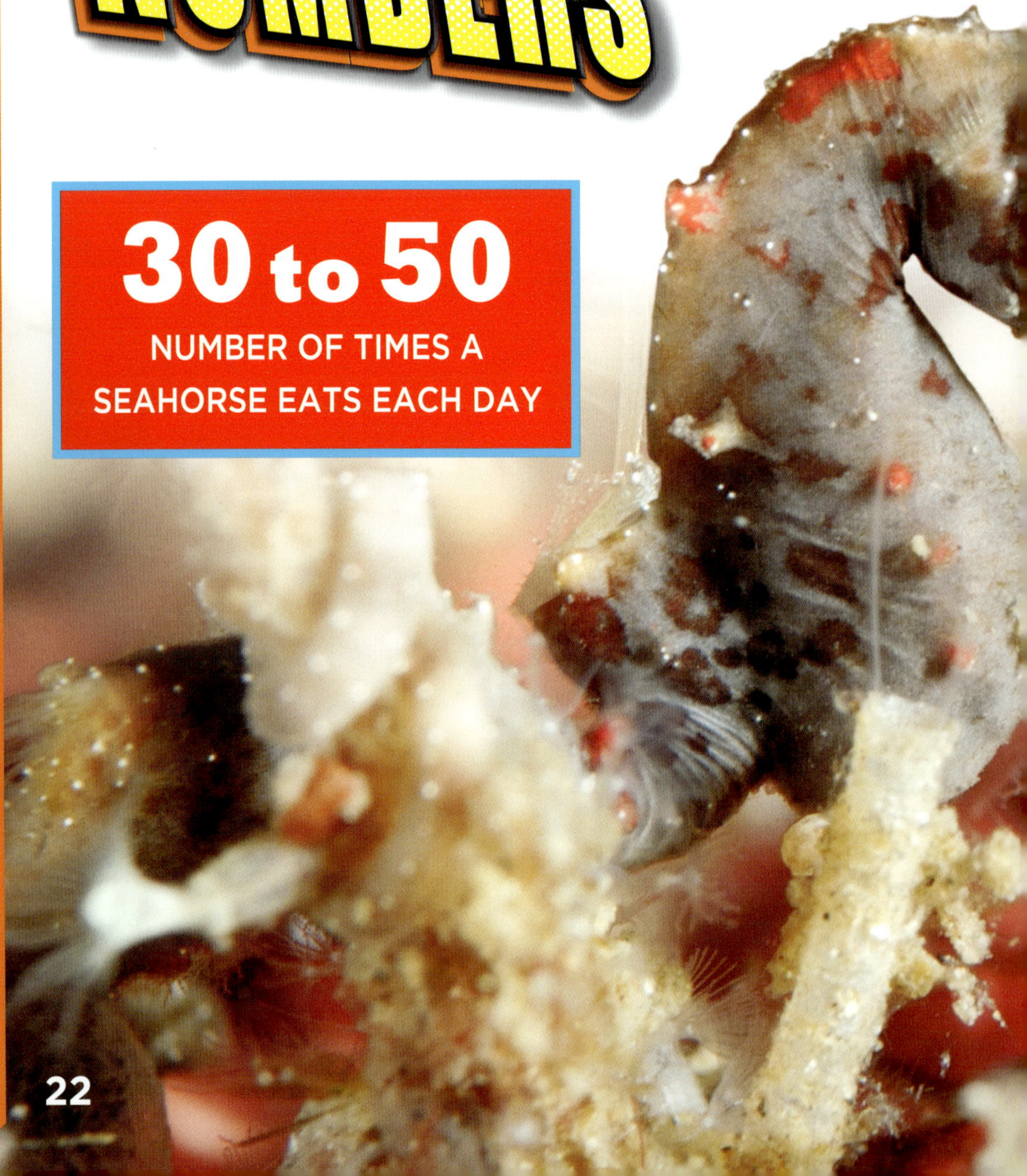

30 to 50

NUMBER OF TIMES A SEAHORSE EATS EACH DAY

UP TO **1,500** HOW MANY BABIES MALES CAN HAVE AT ONE TIME

30 to 70 times a second

HOW FAST THE BACK FIN MOVES

1 to 5 years

LIFE SPAN

Seahorse Food Chain

This food chain shows what eats seahorses.
It also shows what seahorses eat.

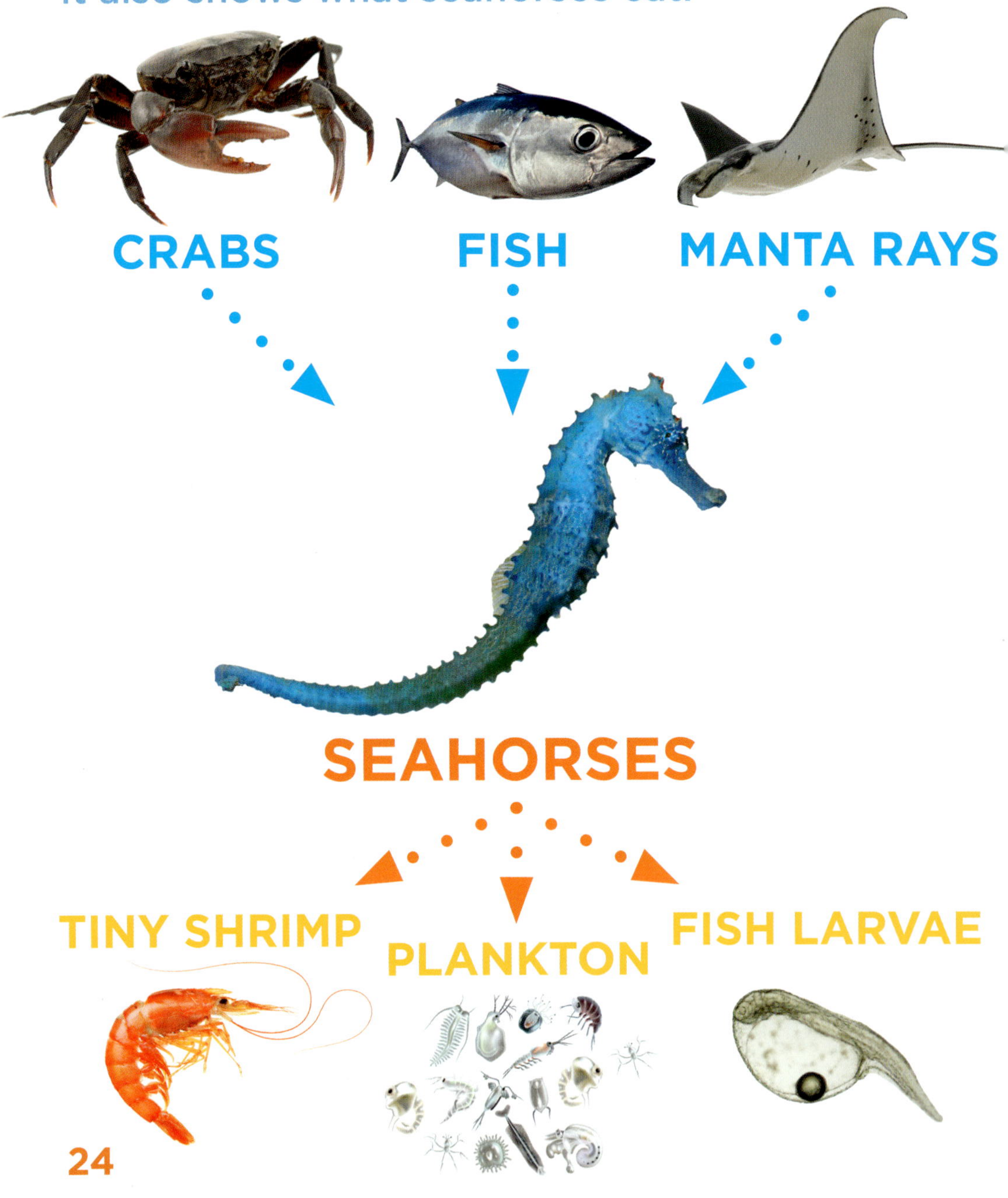

CHAPTER 4

Part of THEIR WORLD

Seahorses have many predators. Crabs and fish eat seahorses. Manta rays do too. Predators have a hard time finding seahorses, though. These small animals can blend right in with their surroundings. Seahorses' bony plates can help keep animals from eating them too.

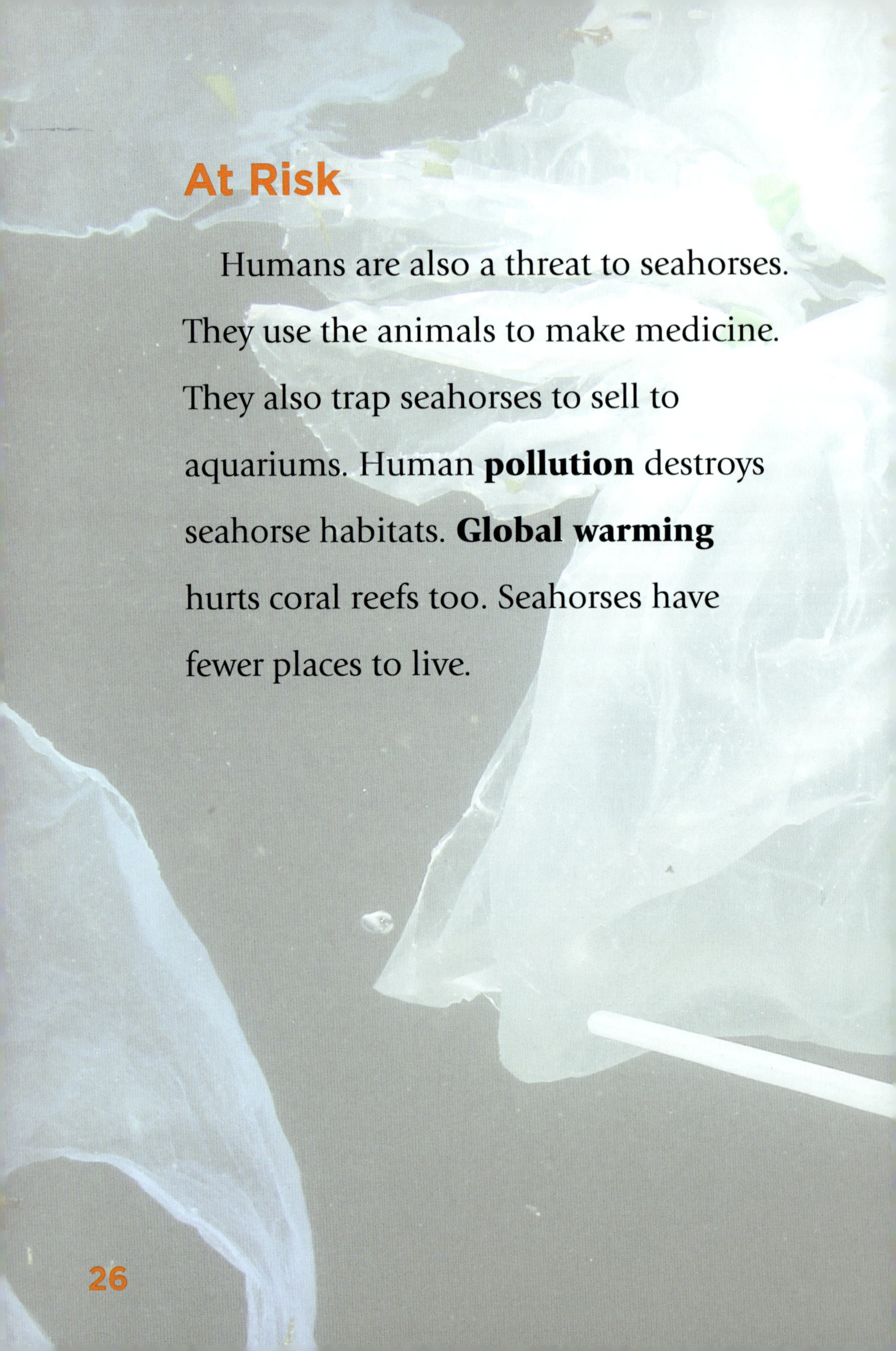

At Risk

Humans are also a threat to seahorses. They use the animals to make medicine. They also trap seahorses to sell to aquariums. Human **pollution** destroys seahorse habitats. **Global warming** hurts coral reefs too. Seahorses have fewer places to live.

Important Animals

Some kinds of seahorses are in danger of dying out. Humans need to protect these animals. Seahorses are important to ocean habitats. They eat many small animals. Seahorses are food for other animals too. They truly are super sea creatures.

GLOSSARY

brood pouch (BROOD POUCH)—the sac of an animal where the eggs are received and develop

fertilize (FUR-tl-ahyz)—to make an egg able to grow and develop

global warming (GLO-buhl WARM-ing)—a warming of Earth's air and oceans

larva (LAR-vuh)—the wormlike form of an animal after hatching from an egg

mate (MAYT)—to join together to produce young

plankton (PLANK-tun)—the very small animal and plant life in an ocean, lake, or river

pollution (puh-LOO-shun)—substances that make land, water, or air dirty and not safe to use

predator (PRED-uh-turh)—an animal that eats other animals

prey (PRAY)—an animal hunted or killed for food

swim bladder (SWIM BLAD-er)—the sac of a fish that contains gas

territory (TER-uh-tor-ee)—an area that is occupied and defended by an animal or groups of animals

LEARN MORE

BOOKS

Bodden, Valerie. *Seahorses.* Amazing Animals. Mankato, MN: Creative Education, 2019.

Bozzo, Linda. *How Seahorses Grow Up.* Animals Growing Up. New York: Enslow Publishing, 2020.

Proudfit, Benjamin. *Seahorses.* Ocean Animals. New York: Gareth Stevens Publishing, 2020.

WEBSITES

Amazing Facts about Seahorses
onekindplanet.org/animal/seahorse/

Seahorse Facts for Kids
www.dkfindout.com/us/animals-and-nature/fish/seahorses

Seahorse Facts for Kids
www.natgeokids.com/au/discover/animals/sea-life/seahorse-facts/

INDEX